LINDERHOF PALACE

OFFICIAL GUIDE

edited by

GERHARD HOJER

and

ELMAR D. SCHMID

with a contribution by

MANFRED STEPHAN

1998

Bayerische Verwaltung der staatlichen Schlösser,
Gärten und Seen, Munich

Edited by Gerhard Hojer and Elmar D. Schmid based on the texts of the Official Guides by Hans Thoma and Michael Petzet, which are derived substantially from Heinrich Kreisel's Official Guide, Linderhof Palace, Munich 1938.
Translation by Malcolm Leybourne.

The section on the gardens was revised by Manfred Stephan.

Fotos: Bayer. Verwaltung der staatl. Schlösser, Gärten und Seen; Martin Herpich OHG, München; Werner Neumeister, München; Bildarchiv Huber, Garmisch-Partenkirchen. Illustrationen S. 3, 48: „Gartenlaube" 1886, S. 633, 648/49. – Verzeichnis der Künstler und Kunsthandwerker O. Weiß.

For further information:

Heinrich Kreisel: Die Schlösser König Ludwigs II. v. Bayern, Darmstadt 1955. – Werner Richter: Ludwig II., König von Bayern, 4. Aufl., München 1956. – Michael Petzet: König Ludwig II. und die Kunst, München 1968 (mit ausführlichen Quellenangaben und Bibliographie). – Wilfrid Blunt: König Ludwig II. von Bayern, München 1970. – Monika Bachmayer: Schloß Linderhof, phil. Diss. München 1977. – Gerhard Hojer: Ludwig II. of Bavaria: Royal Patron of Architecture, in: Designs for the Dream King, Ausst. London u. New York 1978/79. – Michael Petzet und Werner Neumeister: Die Welt des Bayerischen Märchenkönigs, München 1980. – Gerhard Hojer und Horst H. Stierhof: Schloß Linderhof – ein Königstraum wird Wirklichkeit, München 1983. – Rolf Gottwald und Horst H. Stierhof: Ludwigs Schlösser, Hamburg 1986. – Katalog des König Ludwig II.-Museums Herrenchiemsee (hg. von Gerhard Hojer), München 1986. – Stefan Koppelkamm: Exotische Architekturen im 18. und 19. Jahrhundert, Katalog der Ausstellung: Exotische Welten – Europäische Phantasien in Stuttgart, Berlin 1987. – Gerhard Evers: Ludwig II. von Bayern, Theaterfürst, König, Bauherr, München 1986. – J. Fehle: Der Maurische Kiosk in Linderhof v. Karl v. Diebitsch, München 1987. – Detta und Michael Petzet, Die Hundinghütte König Ludwigs II., München 1990.– Elmar D. Schmid: König Ludwig II. im Portrait, Dachau/München 1996.

Linderhof, Illustration by Heinrich Breling, 1886

KING LUDWIG II AND LINDERHOF

1n 1864 when the eighteen year of Crown Prince Ludwig ascended the Bavarian Royal Throne as King Ludwig II, a lonely and joyless youth lay behind him. Temperament and education had made him a dreamer; fantastic scenes from the historical past, of German epics and exotic lifestyles had alienated him to an ever greater degree from the real world. Deep disappointments shaped his character: in 1865, Richard Wagner, whose stage creations represented the realization of Ludwig's dreams, had to leave Munich against the king's will; in 1866, Bavaria became involved in the war against Prussia and came out as loser; in 1867, the king's betrothal came to an unhappy end; and in the same year, construction of the Richard Wagner Festival Hall, designed by Gottfried Semper, was stopped. This rejection also ended the urban project of a street toward the Isar River, which could have assumed an equal rank with Ludwigstrasse and Maximilianstrasse. It is no wonder that King Ludwig II from this time on lost all interest in building projects for the Residence City of Munich.

Ludwig shared his father's and grandfather's royal building passion; since the city had denied him major building projects, he sought the solitude of the mountains for realization of his building plans and building fantasies. As a matter of fact, he commissioned erection of Neuschwanstein Castle as early as 1867. Inspired by a visit to the Wartburg in that year, he desired in a way to recreate the world of Richard Wagner's "Tannhäuser" there.
His visit to Versailles in the same year provided him with the im-

King Ludwig II, portrait by Ferdinand Piloty, 1865 ▶

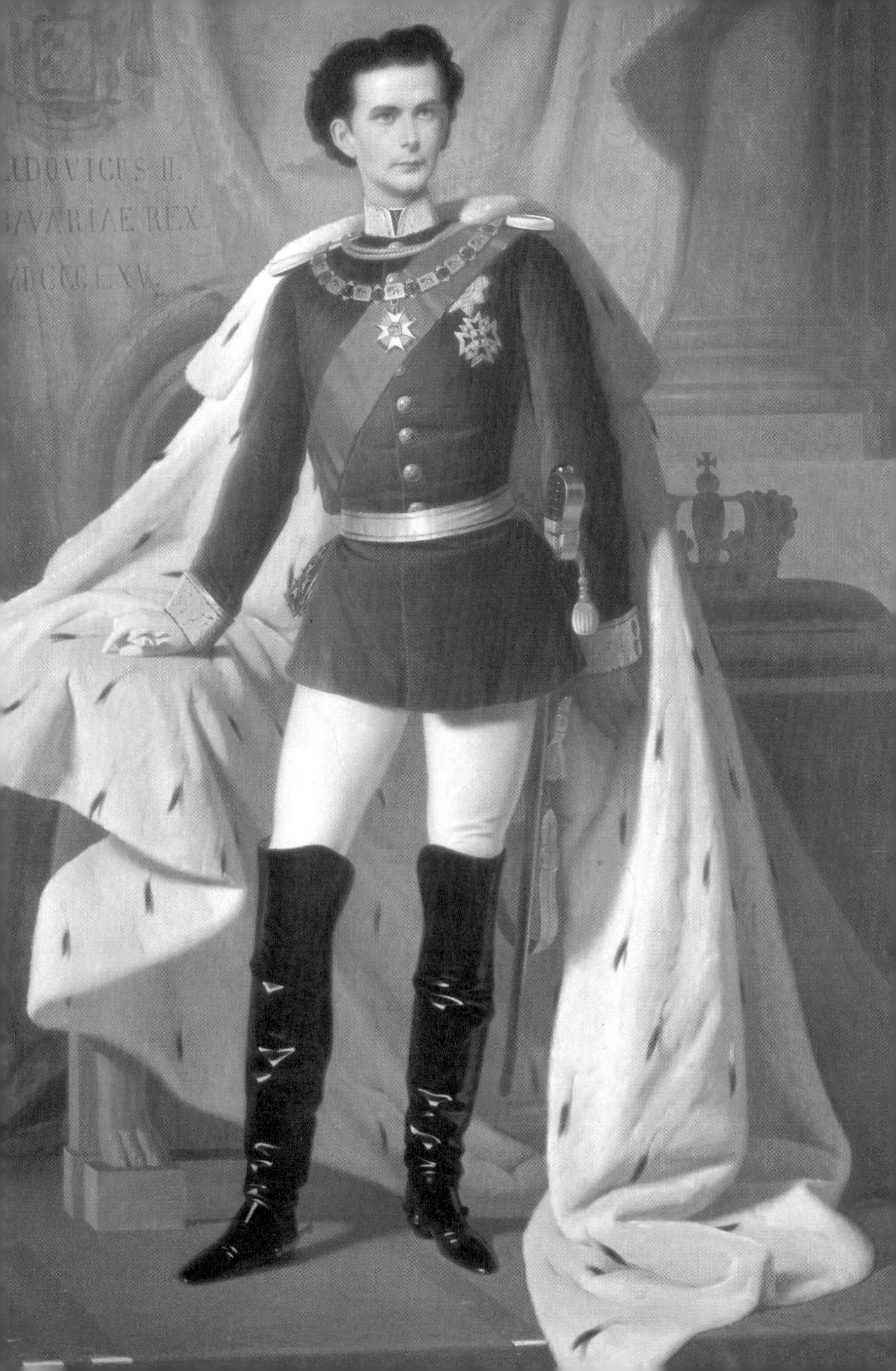

LDOVICUS II.
BAVARIAE REX

pulse to have plans made for a new Versailles Palace. In contrast to his father, he regarded the constitutional monarchy as an intolerable contradiction to his idea of absolute rule; since he was unable to restore absolutism, he desired to erect an architectural monument to it.

This building memorial was to be called "Meicost Ettal", anagram for Louis XIV's motto "L'état c'est moi". In 1868/69, the architect Georg Dollmann designed seven projects for the new Versailles in Linderhof, and it was not until 1870 that Herrenchiemsee Island was designated as the definitive location for the structure. Simultaneously with this project, the king had plans prepared for a gigantic Byzantine palace, likewise in Linderhof, which were never carried out. Instead of this, Ludwig built a "royal villa", which also remained unique as structural type among the "Royal Palaces".

Linderhof does, however, preserve the Versailles idea, even if translated into the private, if not to say the domestic sphere: In extent it is the most modest of the king's palaces, and the only one whose completion he lived to see and in which he resided long and frequently. It is only here, in contrast to Herrenchiemsee and Neuschwanstein, that the coat of arms of the Kingdom of Bavaria is present on the façade, as well as repeatedly in the interior. Here also, he felt himself to be the "Sun King": The copy of an equestrian statue of Louis XIV and his motto "Nec pluribus impar" are in the vestibule. This programmatic reference to Louis XIV is not accidental: Ludwig II was able to trace his name to the Bourbons, for his grandfather and godfather Ludwig I had been lifted from the baptismal font by King Louis XVI of France in Strasbourg in 1786.

Linderhof was not intended to be a structure for representation, but rather, inspired perhaps by the Trianon of Versailles, a retreat in which the monarch could experience the dreamt past as present.

◄ *Castle and main parterre, view from the terrace* 7

The numerous small buildings surrounding Linderhof originate from the same idea, embodiments of the king's imaginative faculty: In the midst of the solitude of the Graswang Valley, he sought while smoking a chibouk in the "Moorish Kiosk; and in the "Moroccan House" to revive the fairytale world of the "Arabian Nights"; in "Hunding's Cabin" (now destroyed) lying on bearskins with his retainers and drinking mead, he wanted to re-experience the mythical content of the "Walküre"; in the golden skiff on the lake of the "Venus Grotto" he desired to feel the enchantment of "Tannhäuser" and on the morning of Good Friday to sense the consecrating effect of "Parsifal" in "Gurnemanz's hermitage" (destroyed). Like the enchanted prince in the fairytale, he rode in the golden rococo sleigh to Linderhof accompanied by coachmen, outriders and lackeys attired in rococo costumes.

ARCHITECTURAL HISTORY

In addition to Schwangau, familiar to him from childhood experience, Ludwig II had become acquainted as crown prince with the Graswang Valley on repeated excursions from Hohenschwangau. His father, King Max II., owned a hunting lodge in "Linderhof". This "Linderhof" was in the 15th century a tithe property of the Ettal Monastery, named after the Linder family which managed it. The name is derived from an ancient linden tree, which – even today – still stands remarkably unsymmetric in the otherwise strictly axially laid out garden, carefully tended and provided with a hunter's seat at the king's request.

Maintenance of the property, hallowed as it was by tradition, also characterized the first project for Linderhof Palace: After acquisition of the land surrounding the hunting lodge of Maximilian II in 1869, the king initially desired only to add an oval salon flanked by two horseshoe-shaped rooms on the northern side of the hunting lodge, as is evidenced by a letter dated 30th September 1870 with a sketch of the Senior Equery Hornig. In the same year, an expanded plan originated, this time by Georg Dollmann, builder of the Giesing Church, private architect of the king from 1868, court building director from 1875, and senior court building director from 1875, and senior court building director from 1881. This plan connects the royal lodge with a U-shaped building complex surrounding a courtyard, which now repeats the suite of rooms foreseen in the first project on the opposite side. The king's bedchamber is located in the middle of the complex to the north, facing the mountain slope; it no longer remains in the royal lodge as in the first sketch of 30th September. On the contrary: it is not only characterized by its central position, it is now the largest room of all. The Versailles model is apparent, and as clear proof for the dependence, in Versailles as in this Linderhof design, the royal state bed is on the outer wall of the chamber with a view toward the courtyard.

This structure, like the royal lodge, a wooden post and beam construction on a plastered base story in old Bavarian style was completed in 1872 and stood for two years. In 1874, the royal lodge was torn down and moved to its current location. At the same time, Linderhof Palace was given its present appearance by addition of the vestibule and the staircase in the courtyard that had previously been open, and above it the hall of mirrors and the "tapestry chambers", but primarily by cladding the previous wooden exterior with stone façades. Since at that time the railroad line ended at Weilheim, all materials for the construction work had to be tediously transported from there to the Graswang Valley. Despite these outer difficulties, the construction was speeded up extremely at the king's express command. The palace was completed in 1878, again under supervision of the architect Georg Dollmann, who later also built Herrenchiemsee.

The "Royal Villa" as the small refuge of the unsociable king, appointed in the style of the 18th century, was called at first, unlike Herrenchiemsee, was not a copy of an already existing building; the "Petit Trianon" palace in the Versailles Park, which may have provided the first inspiration, is scarcely of more significance for Linderhof than as a type. There are, however, direct predecessors of a summer palace with surrounding park in the mountains: aside from the fact that the Austrian Emperor had already had his residence built in Bad Ischl in the midst of an English landscape garden against a magnificent mountain background, Villa Berg in Stuttgart in particular appears to have served as a model for the

Southern garden parterre with fountain ▶

layout of Linderhof; this villa was erected between 1845 and 1853 for Queen Olga of Württemberg. The interior decoration in the "Style of Louis XV" had already been realized as early as 1842 in the Liechtenstein Palace in Vienna; Leon Feuchère published engraved wall details of the "Pompadour Style" in his book "L'Art Industriel" in the same year. This book was in the library of King Ludwig II.

Contrary to the previously held opinion, the sketches for the interior appointments in the style of "Louis XV" are the work of the architect G. Dollmann; they have been preserved in wall developments. Individual designs, for example for entire ceilings were supplied by the stage designer Christian Jank; many details originate from Franz Seitz, Director of the Munich Court Theater, who had already designed a large part of the interior decorations for Ludwig's apartments in the Munich Residence. Adolph Seder designed parquet floor inlays and mantelpieces as well as a large part of the furniture and porcelain. Research must still be conducted to determine to what extent elevations and details of the interiors by Julius Lange, Joseph de la Paix and Ferdinand Knab simply translate ideas of the architects into colored views or represent independent creations.

Although the palace had already been completed in 1878, the king commissioned his architect Julius Hofmann, who had replaced Georg Dollmann, in 1884 to make substantial changes: the royal bedchamber was expanded and refurnished according to Hofmann's plans under the supervision of Eugen Drollinger. At the time of the king's death in 1886, this had not yet been finished and was completed in 1887 in simplified form.

Parallel to the construction work, the large, extraordinarily artistically designed palace garden was laid out under the supervision of K. Effner, which, abundantly adorned with sculptures, was completed in 1880. Following baroque models, the king intended to decorate these gardens and in addition the adjoining forest areas with architectural monuments.

The first of these edifices is the "Moorish Kiosk" which had been purchased in 1876 (p. 45). It was complemented with the "Moroccan House" in the upper Graswang Valley, erected in 1878–1879; it was sold in 1886 and later displayed in Oberammergau; it has recently been re-purchased by the Bavarian Palace Administration to be re-erected in a few years. Among these exotic monuments are the theater sceneries borrowed from Richard Wagner's music dramas. Only the "Venus Grotto" (p. 43) erected in 1876–77 on the southern slope of the Hennenkopf as monumental stage scene from "Tannhauser" remains intact. "Hunding's Cabin" built at the same time, that realistic reproduction of the scenery from "Walküre" (after the stage design by Chr. Jank for the première in 1869) in the midst of the solitude of the Alpine forest as well as the neighboring Gurnemanz hermitage located in a "blossoming Good Friday meadow" (3rd Act of Wagner's "Parsifal") were destroyed in late April 1945 by fire and plundering. All the other park structures planned by the king are known to us only from plans, drawings, water colors or models. Projects from 1875 are preserved to us for an "Arabian Pavillion" and for a palace chapel in baroque style (by F. Knab and G. Dollmann). Plans were made by the same artists starting in 1871 for a theater modelled on the old Residence Theater in Munich (erected by Fr. Cuvilliés the elder in 1751–53 and restored in 1955–58), which was intended to permit the king to have his "private performances" in Linderhof as well. Again following a model by Cuvilliés, the Amalienburg in Nymphenburg Park, a summer residence, the "Hubertus Pavilion" (from the design by J. Hofmann), was projected on the other side of the border on Tyrolean territory; after 1886, the already standing skeleton structure was torn down. Two gigantic projects designed by Hofmann in the year of Ludwig II's death, an early medieval fortress complex in the Graswang Valley and a Chinese palace on the Plansee are the final evidence of the restless fantasy of the king.

THE PALACE STRUCTURE

The main story, richly articulated by windows, figures, banded pilasters, window crowns and trophies over the niches, is supported on a base story constructed of rusticated blocks and enclosed by a balustrade. The three middle axes of the main façade stand out prominently as projection. The balcony of this projection is supported by hermae on the ground floor which flank three semicircular arched portals; in the upper story, two semicircular windows at the sides of an equally high figure niche correspond to the portals. Composite banded freestanding columns flank the openings, behind their impost crowned with figures rises an attic with bull's-eye windows. This attic is closed with a curved gable on which free figures stand and whose tympanium contains a relief of the Bavarian coat of arms held by genii.

The long flanks of the structure facing east and west belong as aspect sides to the parterre on either side. The façade division corresponds in principle to that of the main façade. The projection of the oval room bulging polygonally outwards on each side is shifted from the center of the façade, however, because of the two unsymmetrically added southern axes. The central niche of the projection polygon closed by attic and gables does lie however in the middle axis of the lateral garden parterre.

On the north façade facing the mountain, likewise divided by banded pilasters, rectangular windows and small figure niches, the greatly projecting three-axis structure of the bedchamber is elevated by an attic story corresponding to the front with pilasters and oval false windows.

Main façade: The gilded wrought iron door and balcony grate by P. Kölbl. – Stone sculptures here and on the other façades of Lorrainese limestone (Savonnières): In the middle "Victoria" by Fr. Walker; at the sides of the central projection by Ph. Perron and Th. Bechler: "Teaching Profession", "Profession of Arms", "Jurisprudence" and "Agriculture". – Cast zinc figures: The Atlas figure crowning the gable by Fr. Walker, the remaining figures by Ph. Perron. – Figures on the imposts: two genii with laurel wreaths (above the middle columns) and two pairs of putti above the lateral twin columns ("Music", "Poetry", "Sculpture" and "Architecture"). In the gable: coat of arms of the Kingdom of Bavaria, flanked by two tuba-playing Fama figures. Next to the gable: "Tillage" and "Commerce" – "Science" and "Industry".

Stone figures of the other façades: East façade: "Venus" (by Fr. Walker) – "Wealth" and "Peace". – West façade: "Apollo" (by Fr. Walker) – "Poetry and Music" – Rear façade: "Constancy", "Justice", "Magnanimity" and "Strength" (by Ph. Perron and Th. Bechler).

THE PALACE ROOMS

1 VESTIBULE: The columns and pilasters of the low, flatceilinged room are made of Adneth "red-speckled" marble. The gilded stucco works of the ceiling display a solar head in a halo with the motto of the Bourbons "NEC PLURIBUS IMPAR" ("Equal even against many"). Likewise referring to the Bourbons is the bronze equestrian *statuette,* a reduced reproduction of the statue of Louis XIV of France, which the City of Paris commissioned François Girardon to erect on the Place Vendôme in 1699. On the black marble base Latin inscriptions with the coats of arms of France and Paris of gilded bronze.

2 STAIRCASE: The columns and pilasters in the antechamber are of Adneth "Red Urbano", the wall cladding consists of southern French "Jaune du Var" marble (from the vicinity of Nice). The two-winged stair developing from the middle flight is a reduced recollection of the "Ambassador's Staircase" of the Palace of Versailles. The steps are of Carrara marble and the columns and pilasters of the main story of Adneth "Red Urbano" marble. – The gilded sculptures were designed by Ph. Perron. The glazed skylight of the staircase, repeated on a larger scale in Herrenchiemsee, is a typical structural form of the second half of the 19th century and is evidence of modern advances taken into consideration in the buildings of Ludwig II despite all reversion to structural forms of previous eras.

The *vase* in the antechamber with the representations of "Esther and Ahasverus" by Elise de Maussion (after J. de Troy) comes from the Sèvres Manufactory and is said to have been a present from Emperor Napoleon III to King Ludwig II. – At the beginning of the stairs, two crowned *lion figures* stand holding the Bavarian lozenge coat of arms. Next to them are two *Cloissoné vases,* China, 19th century with rich colored ornamentation in Cloissoné enamel technique.

3 WESTERN TAPESTRY CHAMBER (Music room). It was designed by G. Dollmann in 1874. The dominating theme of the room is the "Gallant festivals", particularly those as painted by A. Watteau early in the 18th century. Consequently, the social and pastoral scenes of the huge murals are also borrowed from his representations, which are painted on coarse canvas to give the impression of woven tapestries. They originate from H. von Pechmann and show "Floral Sacrifice at the Altar of Amor", "Social Gathering in the Open", "Shepherd couple at the Fountain" and "Shepherdess with Bagpipe Player". The gilded carvings of the paneling are a work by Ph. Perron and show emblems of bucolic life: tillage and sheep husbandry on a background of lozenges – a reference to Bavaria. Putti stucco groups over the doors (signed by Schmidt) symbolize the arts "Music", "Painting" and "History". The ceiling painting by W. Hauschild represents Apollo welcoming Venus in the shell chariot accompanied by putti and Water nymphs, an allegory of "Evening". – Inlaid floor. – Mantelpiece (with gilded bronze appliqués) and doorcasing of Tegernsee marble.·

Appointments: Aeolodion, a musical instrument combining piano and harmonium, the housing originates from Ph. Perron after a design by A. Seder of 1871, the mechanism form the Schramm Company in Munich. – The lifesized peacock of painted porcelain comes from the Sèvres Manufactory. – Ph. Perron created the "Apotheosis of Louis XIV of France" on the mantelpiece. – The coverings on the carved and gilded seats as well as the draperies were produced in the Parisian Gobelin Manufactory.

4 YELLOW CABINET: Like the other horseshoe-shaped cabinets flanking a central salon, the atmosphere of a room from the era of King Louis XV of France is conjured up here. The delicate coloring of the yellow silken base with embroidered ornaments likewise presented in the "moonlike" silver shade, the carved rocailles on the light blue background of the panels and the silvered stucco pieces in the cavetto of the blue-gray ceiling all fit into the "Louis XV Style". They show allegories of the four continents (in the form of animals) and the four elements as well as the signs of the zodiac. The design for the ceiling comes from Chr. Jank in 1871. – Pier mirrors with *Meissen porcelain wall lighting* fixtures are incorporated into the paneling, the fixtures being painted with colorful pastoral scenes. The draperies are of yellow silk with abundant silver embroidery.

Appointments: The pictures refer also to the world of Louis XV., particularly the picture above the exit door "Embarkment for Cythera Island", painted by B. Fries from an original by A. Watteau. – The pastel portraits by A. Gräfle with carved and silvered frames after a design by Fr. Seitz depict personalities at the Parisian Court in the rococo era: Duke Maurice of Saxony, Marquise of Créqui, Duke of Belle-Isle and Duchess of Egmont-Pignatelli.

View of the Western Garden Parterre through the window (see page 37).

5 AUDIENCE CHAMBER. The basic design originates from Chr. Jank (1870/71).
Despite the pronouncedly intimate, that is the private character of the Linderhof rooms, King Ludwig II did not want to dispense completely with the central rooms of court ceremonial, since only they visually realized the absolute monarchy. He attached great importance to the Audience Chamber, which finds expression in unusually unequivocal references to the Bavarian Kingdom (in the lunette stucco work by Fr. Walker): The figure of "Bavaria" is re-

presented above the throne baldachin; the Bavarian coat of arms held by Fama figures crowns both doors and the "L" here really referring to Ludwig II appears on the window wall opposite the throne baldachin.

The Bavarian coat of arms in needlework by D. and M. Jörres also forms the central motive of the throne baldachin (design by Fr. Seitz), whose ermine lining allegedly comes from the coronation robe of King Otto of Greece (the uncle of King Ludwig II). The coverings of the carved and gilded seating furniture and the draperies are of green velvet with gold embroidery. Th. Bechler created the stuccowork on the ceiling: emblems of war and peace, music and painting. In the narrow wall sections of the paneling, carved and gilded emblems by Ph. Perron: "Science and Art", "Commerce and Industry", "Worldly Sovereignty" and "Spiritual Sovereignty". The lozenge background points out clearly that this is a glorification of the royal sovereignty in Bavaria. The representation of the four seasons over the doors refers to its temporal dimension: "Spring" and "Summer" (by B. Fries) and on the window wall: "Fall" and "Winter" (by H. von Pechmann). The absolutistic kingdom of the Bourbons is recalled by the lunette pictures: "Versailles" (by Chr. Jank and J. Watter), "Intimate Supper of Louis XV in Versailles" (J. Watter), "Reception of the Turkish Embassy" (by F. Knab and J. Watter) and "Marriage of the Dauphin in the Palace Chapel of Versailles" (R.S. Zimmermann). – The mantelpieces are of Bardiglio marble (from the vicinity of Carrara).

Appointments: Writing ensemble with Bavarian coat of arms from a design by A. Seder of gilded bronze. – On the carved and gilded console of the window side, clock of gilded bronze. – Equestrian statutes of Louis XIV and Louis XV of gilded bronze on marble bases, created by A. Halbreiter from monuments in Paris, which were destroyed in the French Revolution. – Carved and gilded seating furniture from a design by Fr. Seitz; they

are covered with gold-embroidered green velvet, which is also the material of the draperies. – Two round tables with malachite tops, gift of the Czarina Marie Alexandrowna to King Ludwig II.

6 LILAC CABINET. The stucco work of the horseshoe-shaped room was designed by Chr. Jank in 1871 and executed by Fr. Walker. Pier mirrors (with Meissen porcelain wall lighting fixtures) are incorporated into the white and gold paneling; the (replaced) silk covering is lilac. The signature Ludwig (here probably that of Louis XV of France) is found in the gilded stuccowork of the cavetto, in between cartouches with figures of the gods: Jupiter, Flora, Mars and Apollo. The emblems of the cavetto symbolize astronomy, tillage, viticulture, the military profession, industry, fine arts and poetry. The painting over the entrance door "Social gathering in the Open" comes from B. Fries. The gold-embroidered coverings of the carved and gilded seating furniture and the draperies are like the (replaced) wall covering also of lilac silk.

Appointments: The four pastel portraits in the richly carved gold frames were painted by A. Gräfle; they represent: Duchess Marie Anne of Châteauroux, King Louis XV of France, Marquise de Pompadour and Duke Etienne François of Choiseul-Stainville.

7 BEDCHAMBER. In 1871, the painter Angelo Quaglio submitted a design in color, which reproduces as a whole the wall decoration from a design by Dollmann, the cavetto from a design of Chr. Jank and the bed of state as well as the embroidery of the panels from an idea by F. Seitz.

Chr. Jank supplied the design for the ceiling fresco in 1871, and probably A. Seder that for the floor. In 1872 the bedroom had already been extended by one bay to the north; it was completely rebuilt by J. Hofmann and E. Drollinger in 1884. In place of a decoration which quite generally imitated the taste of Louis XV, the bedchamber of the "Opulent rooms" in the Munich Residence were taken as direct model. Despite all similarity, in particular of the bed alcove with its magnificent gold embroidery, there remain significant differences: what is particularly noticeable is the appearance of ceiling frescos in Linderhof, which are not present in the Cuvilliés model.

From the three windows facing the north, one has a view of the cascade on the northern slope of the "Hennenkopf".

White Paneling with gilded carvings. The doorcasings are of Italian, and the two mantelpieces (with gilded bronze appliqués) of French marble. The gilded ceiling stuccoworks are by J. Rappa and J. Giobbe: "Meleager and Atalante", "Amor and Psyche" and "Diana and Endymion". The bed alcove is closed off by a carved and gilded balustrade; its rich gold embroidery on blue velvet comes from J. Bornhauser. Of the embroidery of the velvet covering on the bed, made by D. and M. Jörres, only the royal coat of arms (in needlework) had been completed by the king's death. On the rear wall of the bed baldachin, the Bavarian coat of arms with trumpet-blowing genii. The ceiling painting in the main room comes from A. Spiess and represents the apotheosis of Louis XIV; L. Lesker painted the painting above the bed niche; his theme is the "allegory of morning". Two paintings above the doors are by J. Benczur and represent the "Morning Reception" of Louis XIV in the bedchamber at Versailles and the wedding feast of the dauphin in the Hall of Mirrors at Versailles. The other two paintings above the doors were done by K. Otto and represent: "Merry-go-round in the Park of Versailles; and "Evening Reception of Louis XIV".

The console tables and mirror frames on the window piers are of Meissen porcelain (with putti, flowers and wall lighting fixtures) from designs by E. Drollinger.

Appointments: Tremendous glass candelabra with 108 candles from the firm Lobmeyer in Vienna. – Prie-dieu with needlework by D. and M. Jörres with representation of St. George – holy water receptacle. – Floor candelabra (gilded carving work and bronze). – Marble figures (Carrara marble): On the mantelpieces "Abduction of Helen" and "Abduction of Prosperina" (by F. Walker). On the console tables "Apollo of Belvedere" and "Diana of Versailles" (by A. Kaindl). Two Nymphenburg vases with golden background from East Asian models (gilded cast metal bases).

8   PINK CABINET. Former robing room of the king. It is one of the three rooms to the east, which were rebuilt in 1872, and of which the oval dining room in the middle was changed most.

The ceiling painting with the playing amoretti was designed by Ch. Jank and executed by A. Schultze. – Pier mirrors (with *Meissen porcelain wall lighting* fixtures) are set into the white paneling with gilded carvings and consoles. Otherwise, the walls are covered with pink silk. In the cavetto, gilded stuccowork with freehanging flower garlands. –

Appointments: The four pastel portraits (in gilded carved frames) were painted by A. Gräfle. Represented are Beatrice de Choiseul-Stainville, Duchess of Gramont; Augustin de Maupeau, Chancellor of France; Countess Jeanne Marie Dubarry and Duke Caesar Gabriel de Choiseul. – Carved and gilded seating furniture covered with pink figured silk damask.

9   DINING ROOM. The room was given its final form in 1872. The carvings of the paneling in white and gold were created by Ph. Perron. They represent the origin of the products forming the foundation of the princely table: gardening, hunting, fishing and agriculture. The stuccowork on the ceiling is also devoted to this theme, for which preliminary designs were finished by Chr. Jank in 1870–1872 and executed by Th. Bechler. The completely three-dimensional gilded putti groups represent: grain and wine harvest, flower cultivation, gardening, hunting and fishing. The paintings "Flora"

and "Amor and Psyche" set in quatrefoil-shaped stucco frames into the oval of the ceilings come from E. Schwoiser; "Venus and Bacchus" and "Venus with Amor" were painted by A. v. Heckel. In many places, the painting passes over into sculptural detail following baroque example. One of the paintings above the doors, the "Dethronement of Athalia" also comes from A. von Heckel. The other was painted by L. Thiersch; both pictures are oriented on prototypes by J. de Troy. – Wall mirrors with rich carved framing above the two mantelpieces (Tegernsee marble) and over the console table of the window pier.

Appointments: In the middle of the room, disappearing dumb-waiter with Meissen procelain centerpiece. The table can following prototypes in 18th century France be lowered with a lever system to the ground floor and raised again. Thus the king could dine alone without being disturbed by servants. – Designs for the furniture come from Fr. Seitz: richly carved and gilded magnificent buffet; seating furniture with red silk plush, gold-embroidered draperies. – Meissen porcelain candelabra with many branches. – Fr. Brochier supplied the designs for the two boat-shaped gilded bronze vessels on the mantelpieces, which held the king's cutlery. – Marble statuette of the Venus Medici, reproduction by J. Gröber.

10 BLUE CABINET. *Pier mirrors* (with Meissen porcelain lighting fixtures) in the white paneling with gilded carvings, blue silk covering (with gold carving) and picture above the entrance door in the style of F. Boucher by J. Frank "Leda with the Swan". – The gilded stucco figures of the cavetto come from Th. Bechler and represent emblems of music. L. Gebhard created the ceiling painting: Music-making amoretti.

As in the other cabinets, A. Gräfle painted the four *pastel portraits* in gilded carved frames: They represent persons of the French Court under Louis XV: Countess Julie de Molly-Nesle; Louis François Armand Duplessis, Duke of Richelieu (grandnephew ot the famed statesman); Countess Pauline Felicité de Ventimille and Germain Chanvelin.

View from the Blue Cabinet into the Dining Room ▶

11 EASTERN TAPESTRY CHAMBER. The design for the eastern as well as for the western tapestry chamber originated in 1874 and was made by G. Dollmann.

As in the western tapestry chamber, framed pictures painted on coarse canvas in imitation of tapestry are also placed here into the gilded paneling. The carvings of the paneling with the allegories of "War" and "Peace" were done by Ph. Perron. H. von Pechmann painted the murals. They show: "Diana and Endymion", "Boreas Abducts Oreithyia", "Triumphal Procession of Bacchus" and "Europa on the Bull". The putti groups above the doors represent allegories of "Sculpture", "Architecture" and "Astronomy". – The ceiling painting by W. Hauschild with "Apollo and Aurora" symbolizes morning. The stucco figures of the cavetto come from Th. Bechler. The inlaid parquet floor is a work by A. Lindner. The mantelpiece (with gilded bronze ornaments) and the doorcasings are made of black Belgian marble; the mantelpiece mirror is surrounded by a gilded carved frame. – The coverings of the seating furniture and the draperies come from the Parisian Gobelin Manufactory.

Appointments: Life-sized peacock of Sèvres porcelain. – On the gilded pier table, an equestrian statuette of Meissen porcelain representing the Elector August the Strong of Saxony. – On the mantelpiece a marble group of the "Three Graces" (Carrara marble) by Th. Bechler.

12 MIRROR ROOM. It design originated from the cooperation of the architect G. Dollman and the stage painter Joseph de la Paix in 1874. Its model was the Mirror Cabinet in the Opulent Rooms of the Munich Residence, which was elevated to magnificence in Linderhof and a ceiling picture added. The mirror cabinets created for King Ludwig II in Linderhof and Herrenchiemsee represented for the last time a room form which already in the 18th century had been developed to a high degree of perfection in southern Ger-

many (Bamberg, Würzburg, Ansbach, Munich). The huge wall mirrors set into the white-gold paneling, which give the illusion of an endless expanse of rooms, are framed with richly gilded carving (with ornaments, lamp-bearing putti and brackets). Ph. Perron carved the paneling, and he also supplied the design for the sculptural decoration of the ceiling. The two mantelpieces are clad with lapis-lazuli and decorated with gilded bronze ornaments. The paintings over the doors show scenes from French court life in the Age of Absolutism: "Reception of the Venetian Embassy by Louis XV" (by R. Lehmann). – "Riding to Hounds under Louis XV" (by J. Benczur). – In the gilded stucco cavetto, completely sculptured putti groups and cartouches with scenes from the myth of "Amor and Psyche", above it ceiling painting with the representation of the "Birth of Venus". The ceiling picture in the enmirrored niche comes from Fr. Widmann and represents the "Judgment of Paris". –

Appointments: The design of the furniture comes from A. Seder, execution by A. Pössenbacher. – There is only one carved and gilded console table, all other pieces of furniture are veneered with rosewood and decorated with gilded bronze ornaments. The middle table has a top with lapis-lazuli, amethyst quartz and chalcedon inlay work; the Bavarian coat of arms held by genii is executed in glass mosaic. – The desk and the two gaming tables bear porcelain paintings; the latter represent: "Gaming session under Louis XV in the Gallery of Versailles" and "Coronation of Louis XVI in the Cathedral of Reims" (after J.M. Moreau, the younger). – The coverings of the seating furniture and the draperies are made of light blue silken rep interwoven with silver. – The mantelpiece clock on the bookcase was made in the 18th century and was purchased by Ludwig II in Switzerland; its pearwood grain housing is decorated with gilded bronze ornaments. – The porcelain candlesticks on the desk and the writing utensils come from the Meissen Manufactory, the latter represents an enlarged reproduction of the writing utensils of Queen Marie Antoinette of France fabricated in Sèvres. – The two vases on the bookcase with mythological scenes are made of Sèvres porcelain. – The figure of Louis XV (by A. Hess) on the desk is of Carrara marble as are the two groups by Ph. Perron: "Apollo in the Pool of Thetis" and "The Sun Chargers of Apollo".

The carpet under the table in front of the alcove is made of ostrich plumes. – The ivory candelabra above (with 16 branches) was executed by Ph. Perron from a design by J. Hofmann. The crystal candelabra is from the Lobmeyer firm in Vienna.

GARDENS

The gardens at Linderhof, which cover an area of around 50 hectares (125 acres) are designed along the same lines as the bourgeois villa gardens of the late 19th century, although of course far larger and more lavish given the financial possibilities of the royal purse. The main characteristic of this garden design is the use of various style elements. At Linderhof parts of the gardens are in the Baroque style, parts in the style of the Italian Renaissance, and there is a landscaped section with similarities to the English Garden. With its variety of styles Linderhof is one of the finest examples of historicism in garden design.

After it had proved impractical to recreate Versailles at Linderhof, Ludwig II now chose a much more modest French royal palace as his model: Marly le Roi, a „Hermitage" built for Louis XIV near Versailles. However, as in the case of the Versailles project the idea was not to create an exact copy of the original. Along the lines of a modular construction system, Ludwig II only took over certain sections of it, in this case the large water basin in front of the palace and the cascade behind it, and added elements from other gardens.

The Ildefonso vases, for example, which stand in small ornamental flowerbeds north of the palace, are modelled on vases from the palace and garden complex of „La Granja" in Ildefonso, northwest of Madrid. La Granja, built from 1724 on by King Philip V - a grandson of Louis XIV - is located in a high mountain valley remarkably similar to the setting of Linderhof. The only features remaining from the original „Meicost-Ettal" project are the allegorical figures representing the four continents, the four seasons and the four elements, which are all copies of sculptures in the Versailles gardens.

The geometric garden areas fulfil a particular function in Linderhof. Aligned with the four main rooms on the upper storey of the palace, they are as it were a continuation of the architecture, with high hedges and trees obscuring any view of the surrounding countryside. In this way the king could look through the windows or wander in the gardens certain that the dream world of the palace rooms would not be shattered by the sight of the profane natural landscape outside. This concept was later also repeated in Herrenchiemsee, where Ludwig II similarly ruled out any views of the lake or the mountains.

Carl von Effner (1831-1884), who designed the gardens, received the highest mark of esteem from the king for his labours: while the gardens were being laid out between 1872 and 1880 Ludwig promoted his garden architect to court garden director in 1873 and in 1877 gave him an aristocratic title.

PARTERRE GARDENS

With hedge walls, wooden pavilions and pergolas the gardens resemble outdoor state rooms mirroring the main rooms of the palace. The colourful ornamental flowerbeds are particularly attractive, full of thousands of summer flowers in spite of the inclement alpine weather. Stone and gilt metal figures, vases and the enlivening element of water in the form of cascades and fountains all contribute to the decorative effect of these gardens.

WATER PARTERRE (in front of the palace): The water parterre, which is also bordered by hornbeam hedges, is dominated by a large basin with the gilt fountain group „Flora and puttos"; the fountain itself rises almost 30 m into the air, solely through the pressure of the natural gradient. On the short sides of the rectangular garden are mythological and allegorical stone figures and terracotta vases with ornamental plants; two cast zinc lions guard the bottom of the terrace steps.

Garden sculptures: Fountain group "Flora and putti" (gilded cast zinc) by M. Wagmüller. – Stone sculptures (Lorrainese limestone) by J. Hautmann: "Diana" and "Venus" (1875) on the revetment wall of the palace terrace; Allegories of "Night" and "Day" (1876) on the southern end of the hedgerows.

WESTERN PARTERRE: The first part of the garden to be laid, this is located in front of the audience room of the palace, and dates from 1872. Surrounded by hornbeam hedges it has colourful flowerbeds and boxwood trees, and at the centre a quatrefoil basin with the gilt figure of „Fama"; at the western end is a small fountain with a gilt sculpture „Amor with dolphins". In the hedge niches on the long sides of the garden and in front of two pavilions on the short sides are allegorical stone figures representing the four seasons; in the middle pavilion is a larger than life-sized terracotta bust of King Louis XIV of France and the garden is also decorated with majolica vases crowned with puttos.

Garden sculptures and ornamental vases: Gilded cast zinc figures by F. Walker: "Amor with dolphins" by M. Wagmüller. – Stone figures (Lorrainese limestone) by J. Hautmann. – Majolika vases (from the Nymphenburg Manufactory) from originals of the Choisy-le-Roi Manufactory near Paris.

EASTERN PARTERRE: The counterpart of the western parterre with a similar shape and slightly different design is located in front of the palace dining room. The lawns in the middle are bordered with flowerbeds shaped into spiral and palmette patterns at either end. At the centre is a stone sculpture of „Venus and Adonis"; at the east end a fountain basin with a gilt sculpture „Amor shooting an arrow accompanied by putti", on the long side in the hedge niches are stone figures representing the four elements. The wooden pavilion on the short side contains a larger-than-life-sized stone bust of King Louis XVI of France.

„Arrow-shooting Amor", ▶
fountain in the eastern parterre by M. Wagmüller

Behind this a flight of steps leads to a circular space surrounded by beech espaliers with a star-shaped flowerbed at the centre.

Garden sculptures: Stone figures (Lorrainese limestone) by J. Hautmann. – Fountain group (gilded cast zinc) by M. Wagmüller.

TERRACE AND CASCADES (GARDENS)

Motifs from Italian Renaissance gardens were very popular in the Victorian gardens created in England from approximately 1840 on, in particular the terrace gardens which formed a part of numerous „Italianate Gardens". In 1854 Carl von Effner had the opportunity to study this development during a six-month period of training in England, which was probably where he drew his inspiration for the Terrace Gardens in Linderhof. The slope known as the „Linderbichl" south of the Water Parterre provided the ideal topographical conditions for terracing. The cascade was probably modelled on examples of this feature in the previously-mentioned gardens of „Marly le Roi" in France or „La Granja" in Spain.

TERRACE GARDENS: Two symmetrical flights of steps lead up to the terraces on the Linderbichl. In a semicircular niche on the landing of the first flight is a fountain consisting of three basins and the figures of water nymphs. At the top of the first terrace, where the balustrades end in the figures of two reclining nymphs (in cast metal), are two ornamental flowerbeds with boxwood trees, each with a bell-shaped fountain. In the wall rising behind this terrace is a hall-shaped niche with a larger-than-life-sized bust of Queen Marie Antoinette of France in the middle arch. The top of the second terrace is also decorated with lavish ornamental flowerbeds. The terrace gardens are crowned by a

◀ *Cascade with Neptun fountain*

round temple, originally intended to contain an Apollo statue, but eventually furnished instead with a larger-than-life-sized marble figure of Venus with two amoretti. For a time there was a plan to build a theatre on the site of the temple.

To the right of the lower terrace is the lime tree, around 300 years old, that gave the original tithe farm on this site and hence the palace its name.

Garden sculptures: Naiad fountain (cast zinc): Design by M. Wagmüller, executed (in 1876) in the Maffei Foundry in Munich. – Stone bust (Lorrainese limestone) of Queen Marie Antoinette: on the base, coat of arms of Bourbon-Navarre, Medusa head with Bourbon motto and initials of the queen.

Circular temple: Design by G. Dollmann in 1875. Fluted marble columns with Corinthian capitals, coffered dome, copper roof with gilded central acroterium. – Venus statue (Carrara marble) by J. Hautmann 1877.

The *terrace garden* was completely renovated in 1977–80.

NORTHERN SLOPE WITH CASCADE: Directly behind the palace, steep slopes lead up to the "Hennenkopf". The central axis of the strucutre – to the south continued in the parterre and terrace gardens – is characterized to the north by a cascade of thirty marble steps accompanied by stone vases and two cast amoretti pairs. Above the basin lying at the beginning of the cascade, a pavilionlike arbor corresponding to the circular temple of the southern terrace garden and serving as observation point. The bottom end of the cascade is formed by a stone basin with a water-spouting Neptune group of cast metal. In front of it, a huge ornamental flowerbed in the form of a Bourbon lily flanked by two stone vases. Linden pergolas (with pavilions above and allegorical stone figures of the four continents below) lead from the beginning of the cascade in broadly sweeping quadrants to the ends of the lateral palace parterres.

St. Anna Chapel, interior ▶

Stone sculptures an ornamental vases: The cast zinc works from the designs of M. Wagmüller. The Neptune group after a prototype in Versailles; originally intended for the basin of the main parterre and not transferred to its current position until 1882. – The ornamental vases of the cascade by Ph. Perron, th so-calles Ildefonso vases (Lorrainese limestone) on the stone basin after the original in the park of San Ildefonso near Madrid.

LANDSCAPE GARDEN

The last major European garden style, initiated in England in the 18th century, was an attempt to reproduce in an idealized form the picturesque romantic atmosphere of the natural landscape. In Southern Germany gardens of this type were created first at Schwetzingen and Schönbusch and then in Munich with the English Garden.

The palace park in Linderhof is an example of the later type of landscape garden. The paths trace the slopes of the deep circular valley almost as smoothly as if drawn by a compass. Where they fork, thick clumps of trees consisting of beeches, lime trees and oaks all over a hundred years old provide shady spots which alternate with expansive, sunny meadows. The ingenious interplay of curving paths, groups of trees and meadows provides the visitor with constant scenic variety on a walk through the park, with the mountains of the Ammergau range forming an impressive backdrop.

 Venus Grotto

King Ludwig II. in the Venus Grotto. Illustration by Robert Assmus, 1896

STRUCTURES IN THE PARK

The buildings in the park are not merely decorative as was usual in early landscape gardens where they functioned as an additional focus of interest. They were rather separate refuges or „subsidiary residences", of which Ludwig II had a large number, for example in the form of 11 mountain huts in the area between Lenggries and Füssen. The Royal Lodge and the St Anna Chapel were already standing at Linderhof before the royal buildings were put up and were incorporated in the park.

ROYAL LODGE: The hunting lodge, dating from 1790 and rebuilt by King Maximilian II, originally stood in front of the palace. It was torn down in 1874 and re-erected on its present site. Prior to completion of the palace, it was repeatedly used as residence by Ludwig II and after the death of the king by Prince Regent Luitpold.

ST. ANNA CHAPEL: Built in 1684 by Abbot Roman Schretler of Ettal. Small building wiht ridge turret; cruciform vaulted singelnave interior with round choir closing. Altarpiece "Holy-Family" from the period when it was built. – Stained glass windows: Christ, Mary and the Three Magi. King Louis IX of France and Richard of England, patron saints of Ludwig II and Richard Wagner. Executed in the studio F. X. Zettler in Munich.

VENUS GROTTO: The entrance and exit of this "magic grotto" erected on the slope of the Hennenkopf are reproductions of cliffs. The magically illuminated in various colors artificial stalactite grotto, a ten meter high main grotto and two side grottos, are intended to reproduce the interior of the Hörselberg, scene of the first act of Wagner's "Tannhäuser". The motive of the blue grotto of Capri – here an underground illuminated lake into which a waterfall pours – is connected with this mysterious rocky world. A gilded shell boat, a platform on the "Loreley Cliff" glittering with crystals and a "Royal Seat" with shell-shaped throne gave Ludwig II observation points, from wich he could be inspired by this fantastic dreamworld. Scarcely anywhere else in this remarkable mixture of natural and technical motives are we confronted so movingly with the striving of the king for panoramic and at the same time emotionally filled illusionism than here in this naturalistically contructed stereoscopic stage, in wich the Venus scene from "Tannhäuser" appears in the background in a monumental painting by A. Heckel.

Building history: First design by F. Schabet; execution in 1876/77 by the "landscape sculptor" A. Dirigl. – The structural design consist of piers, vault chords and iron struts; the illusion of rocks and stalactite formations is achieved through canvas and cement with lustrous stibnite. – 24 dynamos supplied the electric current for the original illumination (one of which is preserved in the Deutsches Museum in Munich as one of the earliest memorials of electrical engineering). The alternating light effects were produced by rotating glass disks placed in front of 24 arc lamps. The current illumination is produced by concealed spotlights through an underwater lighting installation.

MOORISH KIOSK: The kiosk has been erected by the Berliner architect Karl von Diebitsch for the International Exhibition in Paris 1867.

In 1870 the railroad king Bethel Henry Strousberg bought the pavilion for his newly purchased castle at Zbirow/Bohemia. After the bankruptcy of Strousberg Ludwig II acquired the building for the Linderhof park and had it rebuilt according to plans by G. Dollmann and partly reappointed. Its construction is composed of an iron- and wood-frame, which is wainscotted on the outer side with coloured zinc-cast sheets. The wainscotting of the inner walls is formed by richly decorated plaster slabs above a wooden base-moulding. The Moorish Kiosk is located high up on two terrace levels. A colourful, exotic arrangement of palms, pomegranate trees and numerous flowering shrubs extends the foreign atmosphere of the Kiosk outside the walls and also distinguishes its surroundings from the rest of the park. Between 1972 and 1983

Moorish Kiosk ▶

the kiosk was completely restored: sanitation of the basement-construction, reconstruction of the outer walls' original coloration, roof-restoring, from 1986 to 1987 the breast-walls and the steps of the terrace.

Quadratic plan with three rectangular projections and a semicircular apse (the apse was added by G. Dollmann at Ludwig's II request for the throne-niche). Gilded central dome, four minaretlike corner towers. – Richly decorated, dome-vaulted interior with three rectangular niches and apse-shaped, elevated projection; continous arcades with quadruple columns of cast-iron; flat ceiling with wooden stalactite vault in the middle of the room and in the apse; stained glass windows. – White marble fountain with architectural superstructure in cast zinc; large glass candelabra with 32 colored lamps, matching lanterns in the niches.

Peacock throne, fabricated in 1877 in Paris and Munich for the king; octogonal show table; smoking and coffee tables, stool with feather dusters; Persian thurible in peacock shape, of copper, with inlaid turquoises.

Appointments: Stained glass windows from the Kunstanstalt F. X. Zettler, Munich. – Peacock throne: design by Franz Seitz (1877), peacocks enamelled cast metal (with polished Bohemian glass gems in the tail fans) and bronze-gilded back by LeBlanc-Granger, silk-covered divan by A. Pössenbacher, Munich. Octogonal table: mother-of-pearl inlays in the color-framed top, design by K. von Diebitsch. 12 little tables in the niches also from designs by K. v. Diebitsch.

HUNDING'S HUT

In 1876, King Ludwig II, had the so-called Hunding Hut built at the foot of the Kreuzspitze, with an elevation of 2185 metres the highest peak of the Ammer Mountains, southwest of Schloss Linderhof. This primieval old Germanic lodging is inspired by Richard Wagner's directions for the scene of the action in the First Act of the "Walküre" from the "Ring des Nibelungen". Wagner had described "Hunding's dwelling" as early as in 1852 in the libretto of his "Walküre" as follows: "The interior of a dwelling. The trunk of a mighty ash tree stands in the middle, its greatly protruding roots disappear largely into the ground; the treetop is separated from the trunk by a carpentered roof, which is precisely cut out to permit the trunk and the branches spreading out in all directions to grow through; it is assumed that the leafy treetop spreads out above this roof. A room is built around the ash trunk as centre; the walls are made of rough-hewn timbers, here and there hung with braided and woven covers. In the foreground at the right is the hearth with a chimney proceeding sidewards to the roof: behind the hearth an inner room, like a storeroom is located to which wooden rising steps lead; in front of it hangs a half-folded back plaited cover. There is an entrance door in the background with a simple wooden bolt. At the left a door to an inner chamber, to which ascending steps also lead; further forward on the same side there is a table with a wide bench set into the wall behind and wooden stools in front."

Planning and construction of Hunding's Hut are directly connected with the first complete performance of the music drama "Der Ring des Nibelungen" on the occasion of the first Bayreuth Festival in August 1876. Kind Ludwig II attended the final rehearsals starting on 6th August and the third cycle of the Ring" at the end of the month.

Already on 17th August the king had announced to Hofrat Lorenz von Düfflipp the new building project: "His Majesty intends to

Hunding's Hut, interior ▶

erect near Linderhof a chamber made completely of rough logs, like the decoration of the 1st Act in the Walküre, a search is now being made for the tree. His Majesty believes that this can be built with very low costs, the Hofrat should think the matter over."

The plans drawn up already in August 1876 by Court Architect Georg Dollmann – apparently in cooperation with the Court Garden Architect Karl von Effner – provided for a plain log cabin, which at first glance scarcely differs from the type of forest cabins still in use in the mountains today. The design and model of Christian Jank for the Munich premiere of the "Walküre" performed in 1870 against Wagner's will served as basis for the conception of the hall-like room, in the middle of which is a "double beech with ash trunk surrounding cover" selected by King Ludwig II himself. Some details were also taken over from Joseph Hoffmann's scenery for the Bayreuth Festival performance. On 13th November 1876 Hunding's Hut was already largely completed.

Hunding's Hut was the first completed project "At the Seven Springs" at the foot of the Kreuzspitze. In 1877, the Hermitage of Gurnemanz after Wagner's "Parsifal" (destroyed) followed. The narrow valley with the road from Linderhof to the Plansee was enclosed here in the south by a mountain chain with steep, rocky north side. Numerous larger and smaller streams dig into the rock and in some cases form deep gorges. The king selected the location of Hunding's Hut in this wild, creviced, wooded part of the Ammer Mountains almost certainly considering the "Walküre" as a whole. A "wild rocky range" with a gorge is called for in the Second and the "peak of a rocky mountain" in the Third Act. In "Parsifal" also, the action takes place in the mountains, in a "region in the character of the northern mountains of Gothic Spain."

With Hunding's Hut, Hermitage and the Grotto of Venus (p. 47), King Ludwig II "transplanted" three stage settings from Richard Wagner's music dramas into outdoor nature in the surroundings of his favourite palace Linderhof.

Hunding's Hut was destroyed by fire on 18th December 1884 but by early 1885 was reconstructed by order of Ludwig II at the same place and in the same form. Arson caused the building – which had become a popular excursion goal by then – to go up in flames for the second time in 1945 and it was destroyed down to the foundations. A few decorative pieces – two drinking horns, an antlered candelabra, skins – remained preserved. Planned since 1986, Hunding's Hut was reconstructed from 1989 to 1990 in the original form with the aid of Georg Dollmann's set of drawings from 1876, a view of the room (water colour) by Heinrich Breling from 1882, as well as historical photographic material. The authentically reconstructed and furnished building was placed on the eastern edge of the Schloss Linderhof Park, in a landscape situation, which together with the newly laid out small lake corresponds largely to the original location.

BIOGRAPHICAL DATES IN THE LIFE OF KING LUDWIG II

Ludwig II, the last great builder from the House of Wittelsbach, received his name from his grandfather, King Ludwig I (reigned from 1825 to 1848), on whose nameday he was born. Although personally thrifty, Ludwig I was a patron of the fine arts, a genial ruler, who elevated Munich to a European art center through monumental structures and newly assembled collections. His son, Maximilian II (reigned from 1848 to 1864), a brooding character dedicated to his royal office, married in 1842 Princess Marie of Prussia, mother of Ludwig II and Otto I.

1845, 25th August: Ludwig II born in Nymphenburg Palace in Munich (on the nameday of his grandfather Ludwig I).

1861, 2nd February: Ludwig sees a Wagner opera (Lohengrin) for the first time.

1864, 10th March: Maximilian II deceased, Ludwig II ascends the Bavarian royal throne – 4th May: first meeting of the king with Richard Wagner.

1865, 10th June: Première of "Tristan und Isolde" in Munich Court Theater. – 10th December: Wagner leaves Munich.

1867, 22 January: Betrothal of the King with Princess Sophie (daughter of Duke Maximilian in Bavaria) – 31st may: Trip to the Wartburg. – 20th July: Trip to Paris. – 10th October: Dissolution of the betrothal.

1868, 21st June: Première of the "Meistersinger von Nürnberg" in the Munich Court Theater – First plans for Neuschwanstein.

1869, 5th September: Laying of the cornerstone for Neuschwanstein Palace – 22nd September: Premiére of "Rheingold" in the Munich Court Theater – First plans and start of construction on Linderhof Palace.

1870, 26th June: Première of "Walküre" in the Munich Court Theater – 30th September: First detailed plan for Linderhof.

1872, 6th May: First "separate performance" before the king – 22nd May: Laying of the cornerstone for the Festival House in Bayreuth.

1873, Acquisition of the Herreninsel in the Chiemsee by the king.

1874, 20th August: Trip to Paris.

1876, 10th February: The king at a court banquet for the last time 6th–9th August and 27th–31st August: The king in Bayreuth ("Ring des Nibelungen" in the Festival House).

1878, 21st may: Laying of cornerstone for Herrenchiemsee Palace.

1879, Completion of Linderhof Palace.

1886, 10th June: Regency proclamation (in place of Ludwig II and the incurably ill Prince Otto, Prince Luitpold, a son of Ludwig I, assumes the Regency) – 12th June: Accompanied by psychiatrists, the king is brought from Neuschwanstein to Berg Palace. 13th June: The king drowns in the Starnberger See – Funeral in St. Michael in Munich.

LIST OF ARTISTS
AND ARTISANS

Aßmus, Robert 48
Bechler, Theobald 16, 22, 29, 30, 33
Benczur, Julius 26, 34
Bornhauser, Joseph 26
Breling, Heinrich 3, 57
Brochier, Franz 30
Boucher, François 30
Cuvilliés, François d. Ä. 14
Diebitsch, Karl v. 50, 53
Dirigl, August 50
Dollmann, Georg 7, 9, 10, 13, 14, 20, 25, 33, 44, 53, 56, 57
Drollinger, Eugen 13, 25, 26
Effner, Carl v. 13, 39, 43, 56
Feuchère, Leon 13
Frank, Julius 30
Fries, Bernhard 21, 22, 25
Gebhardt, Ludwig 30
Giobbe, Johann B. 26
Girardon, François 19
Gräfle, Albert 21, 25, 29, 30
Gröber, Joseph 30
Halbreiter, Adolf 22
Hauschild, Wilhelm 20, 33
Hautmann, Johann Nepomuk 40, 43, 44
Heckel, August v. 30, 50
Heß, Anton 34

Hofmann, Julius 13, 14, 25, 37
Hoffmann, Joseph 56
Jank, Christian 13, 14, 21, 22, 28, 29, 56
Jörres, Dora und Mathilde 22, 26, 29
Kaindl, Anton 29
Knab, Ferdinand 13, 14, 22
Kölbl, Peter 16
Lange, Julius 13
Le Blanc-Granger 53
Lehmann, Rudolf 34
Lesker, Ludwig 26
Lindner, A. 33
Lobmeyer 29, 37
Maussion, Elise de 19
Moreau, Jean Michel d. J. 34
Otto, Karl 26
Paix, Joseph de la 13, 33
Pechmann, Heinrich Frhr. von 20, 22, 33
Perron, Philipp 16, 19, 20, 22, 29, 33, 34, 37, 47
Piloty, Ferdinand 4
Pössenbacher, Anton 34, 53
Quaglio, Angelo 25
Rappa, Johann 26
Schabet, Fidelis 50
Schmidt 20

Schramm 20
Schultze, August 29
Schwoiser, Eduard 30
Seder, Adolph 13, 20, 22, 25, 34
Seitz, Franz 13, 21, 22, 25, 53
Semper, Gottfried 4
Spieß, August 26
Thiersch, Ludwig 30
Troy, Jean de 30
Wagmüller, Michael 40, 43, 44, 47

Wagner, Richard 4, 14, 49, 54, 56
Walker, Franz 16, 25, 29, 40
Watteau, Antoine 20, 21
Watter, Joseph 22
Widenmann, Franz 34
Zettler, Franz 49, 53
Zimmermann, Reinhard Sebastian 22

Bayerische Verwaltung der
staatlichen Schlösser, Gärten und Seen

SEHENSWÜRDIGKEITEN

Ansbach	**Residenz der Markgrafen von Ansbach;** Prunkappartements des frühen Rokoko, Sammlung Ansbacher Fayencen und Porzellan, Hofgarten mit Orangerie	Tel. 0981/3186 Fax 0981/95840
Aschaffenburg	**Schloß Johannisburg** Gemäldegalerie und Kurfürstliche Wohnräume, Sammlung von Korkmodellen, Schloßgarten – Städtisches Schloßmuseum	Tel. 06021/22417 Fax 06021/218921
	Pompejanum; Nachbildung eines römischen Hauses und Antikenmuseum	
	Schloß und Park Schönbusch Klassizistisches Schlößchen in englischem Landschaftsgarten	
Bamberg	**Neue Residenz Bamberg** Kaisersaal und barocke Prunkräume, Gemäldegalerie, Rosengarten	Tel. 0951/56351 Fax 0951/55923
Bayreuth	**Neues Schloß** Markgrafenresidenz aus der Zeit des »Bayreuther Rokoko« mit Museum Bayreuther Fayencen, Hofgarten mit Orangerie	Tel. 0921/759690 Fax 0921/7596915
	Markgräfliches Opernhaus	

Bayreuth/ Donndorf	**Schloßpark Fantaisie** Historische Gartenanlage	Tel. 0921/759690 Fax 0921/7596915
Bayreuth/ Eremitage	**Altes Schloß Eremitage** Wohnräume der Markgräfin Wilhelmine, Grotte, historische Gartenanlage mit Wasserspielen	Tel. 0921/759690 Fax 0921/7596915
Bayreuth/ Wonsees Sanspareil	**Morgenländischer Bau** Stilräume, Gartenparterre und Felsengarten **Burg Zwernitz,** Burganlage	Tel. 0921/759690 Fax 0921/7596915
Burghausen	**Burg zu Burghausen** Burganlage, Stilräume, Gemäldegalerie	Telefon und Fax 08677/4659
Coburg	**Schloß Ehrenburg** Historische Wohn- und Prunkräume des Barock und 19. Jahrhunderts	Tel. 09561/80880 Fax 09561/808840
Coburg/ Rödental	**Schloß Rosenau** in englischem Landschaftsgarten, Wohnräume der Biedermeierzeit und neugotischer Marmorsaal	Tel. 09563/4747 Fax 09561/808840
Dachau	**Schloß Dachau;** Festsaal, historische Gartenanlage	Tel. 08131/87923 Fax 08131/78573
Eichstätt	**Willibaldsburg** Festungsanlage, Juramuseum, Ur- und Frühgeschichtsmuseum, Hortus Eystettensis (im Aufbau)	Tel. 08421/4730 Fax 08421/8194
Ellingen	**Residenz Ellingen**; Prunk- appartements des Fürsten Wrede, Deutschordensräume, Schloßkirche, historische Gartenanlage	Tel. 09141/3327 Fax 09141/72953
Garmisch- Partenkirchen	**Jagdschloß Schachen** Wohnräume und Maurischer Saal	Tel. 08821/2996

Herren-chiemsee	**Neues Schloß Herrenchiemsee** Wohn- und Repräsentations-räume, historische Gartenanlage mit Wasserspielen und **König Ludwig II.-Museum**	Tel. 08051/3069 Fax 08051/64646
Kelheim	**Befreiungshalle**	Tel./Fax 09441/1584
Kempten	**Residenz Kempten** Prunkräume und Thronsaal der Fürstäbte	Tel. 0831/256-1 und 0831/256-321 Fax 0831/256-260
Königssee	**St. Bartholomä;** Jagdschloß, Kapelle St. Johann und Paul, Naturpark Berchtesgaden	Tel. 08652/96360 Fax 08652/64721
Kulmbach	**Plassenburg;** Schöner Hof, historische Markgrafenzimmer, Gemäldegalerie, Jagdwaffensammlung	Tel. 09221/4116
Landshut	**Stadtresidenz;** Stilräume und Gemäldegalerie, Kreis- und Stadtmuseum	Tel. 0871/924110 Fax 0871/9241140
	Burg Trausnitz Burganlage mit Burgkapelle St. Georg, Stilräume	
Lauenstein bei Ludwigsstadt	**Burg Lauenstein** Burganlage, Wohnräume, volkskundliche Sammlungen	Tel. 09263/400
Linderhof	**Schloß Linderhof** Wohn- und Repräsentations-räume, Venusgrotte, Maurischer Kiosk und Hundinghütte, historische Gartenanlage mit Wasserspielen	Tel. 08822/3512 Fax 08822/3587
München	**Residenzmuseum** Historische Wohn- und Prunkräume aus der Zeit der Renaissance bis zum 19. Jahrhundert, Hofkirchen	Tel. 089/290671 Fax 089/29067225

und -kapellen, Spezial-
sammlungen (Silber, Porzellan,
Paramente, Reliquien)

Schatzkammer

Altes Residenztheater
(Cuvilliés-Theater)

Hofgarten

Bavaria mit Ruhmeshalle Tel. 089/508725
auf der Theresienhöhe

Schloß Nymphenburg Tel. 089/179080
Prunk- und Stilräume,   Fax 089/17908627
Festsaal, Schönheitengalerie,
Schloßkapelle

**Amalienburg, Badenburg,
Pagodenburg, Magdalenen-
klause** im historischen
Schloßpark

Marstallmuseum
Höfische Kutschen und Schlitten,
Reit- und Sattelzeug

Museum Nymphenburger Porzellan
Sammlung Bäuml

Englischer Garten   Tel. 089/341986
Landschaftsgarten im   Fax 089/335169
englischen Stil

München/ **Neues Schloß Schleißheim** Tel. 089/3158720
Oberschleiß- Festsäle, Staatsappartements, Fax 089/31587250
heim   Gemäldegalerie, barocker
    Hofgarten

    Schloß Lustheim
    Porzellansammlung

Neuburg **Schloßmuseum**   Tel. 08431/8897
a.d. Donau **Neuburg a.d. Donau** Fax 08431/42689
    Sgraffitofassade, Kapelle,
    Grotten; Vorgeschichte
    Pfalz-Neuburg, Kirchlicher
    Barock, Fossilienprägekabinett

Neuschwan-stein/Hohen-schwangau	**Schloß Neuschwanstein** Wohn- und Repräsentations-räume	Tel. 08362/81035 Fax 08362/8990
Nürnberg	**Kaiserburg Nürnberg** Palas, Stilräume, Doppelkapelle, Tiefer Brunnen und Sinwellturm, Burggarten	Tel. 0911/225726 Fax 0911/2059117
Prunn im Altmühltal	**Burg Prunn** Stilräume	Tel. 09442/3323
Übersee/ Feldwies	**Künstlerhaus Exter** mit Atelier des Malers Julius Exter	Tel. 08642/895083 Fax 08642/895085
Utting am Ammersee	**Gasteiger Künstlerhaus** Sommervilla mit Wohnräumen und Werken von Anna und Mathias Gasteiger, Villengarten	Tel. 08806/2682
Veitshöchheim	**Schloß und Park Veitshöchheim;** Historische Wohnräume, Rokokogarten mit Wasserspielen	Tel. 0931/91582
Würzburg	**Residenz Würzburg;** Barocke Prunkräume, Fresken von G.B. Tiepolo, Gemäldegalerie, Hofgarten	Tel. 0931/355170 Fax 0931/51925
	Festung Marienberg Festungsanlage, Fürstenbau-museum mit Schatzkammer, Paramentensaal und stadt-geschichtliche Sammlungen, Maschikuliturm; Mainfränkisches Museum, Fürstengarten	

VERÖFFENTLICHUNGEN DER BAYERISCHEN VERWALTUNG DER STAATLICHEN SCHLÖSSER, GÄRTEN UND SEEN

Amtliche Führer
Deutsche Ausgaben:

Ansbach	Residenz Ansbach
Aschaffenburg	Schloß Aschaffenburg
	Pompejanum in Aschaffenburg
	Schloß und Park Schönbusch
Bamberg	Neue Residenz Bamberg
Bayreuth	Eremitage zu Bayreuth
	Markgräfliches Opernhaus Bayreuth
	Neues Schloß Bayreuth
Bayreuth/Wonsees	Felsengarten Sanspareil – Burg Zwernitz
Burghausen	Burg zu Burghausen
Coburg	Coburg – Schloß Ehrenburg
Coburg/Rödental	Schloß Rosenau
Dachau	Schloß Dachau
Eichstätt	Willibaldsburg Eichstätt
Ellingen	Residenz Ellingen
Garmisch-Partenkirchen	Königshaus am Schachen
Herrenchiemsee	Neues Schloß Herrenchiemsee
Kelheim	Befreiungshalle Kelheim
Königssee	St. Bartholomä am Königssee
Kulmbach	Plassenburg ob Kulmbach
Landshut	Landshut Burg Trausnitz
	Stadtresidenz Landshut
Lauenstein bei Ludwigstadt	Burg Lauenstein
Linderhof	Schloß Linderhof
München	Residenz München
	Schatzkammer der Residenz München
	Altes Residenztheater in München (Cuvilliés-Theater)
	Englischer Garten München
	Ruhmeshalle und Bavaria
	Nymphenburg, Schloß, Park und Burgen
	Marstallmuseum in Schloß Nymphenburg
Neuburg a. d. Donau	Schloßmuseum Neuburg an der Donau
Neuschwanstein/ Hohenschwangau	Schloß Neuschwanstein

Nürnberg	Kaiserburg Nürnberg
Oberschleißheim	Schloß Schleißheim, Neues Schloß und Garten
Prunn	Burg Prunn
Riedenburg	Burg Rosenburg in Riedenburg an der Altmühl
Veitshöchheim	Veitshöchheim
Würzburg	Festung Marienberg zu Würzburg
	Residenz Würzburg und Hofgarten

English Editions:

Aschaffenburg	Aschaffenburg Castle and Pompeiianum
Bayreuth	Margravial Opera House Bayreuth
	The Hermitage at Bayreuth
Coburg	Coburg Ehrenburg Palace
Garmisch-Partenkirchen	The Royal House on the Schachen
Herrenchiemsee	The New Palace of Herrenchiemsee
Linderhof	Linderhof Palace
München	Marstallmuseum Schloss Nymphenburg in Munich
	Nymphenburg, Palace, Park, Pavilions
	Residence Munich
	The Old Residence Theatre in Munich
	The Treasury in the Munich Residence
Neuschwanstein/ Hohenschwangau	The Castle of Neuschwanstein
Nürnberg	Imperial Castle Nuremberg
Würzburg	The Würzburg Residence and Court Gardens

Editions with English Summary:

Bamberg	Neue Residenz Bamberg
Bayreuth/Wonsees	Felsengarten Sanspareil – Burg Zwernitz
Burghausen	Burg zu Burghausen
Coburg/Rödental	Schloß Rosenau
Königssee	St. Bartholomä am Königssee
München	Englischer Garten München
Oberschleißheim	Schloß Schleißheim

Editions Françaises:

Garmisch-Partenkirchen	Le Châlet Royal de Schachen
Herrenchiemsee	Le Nouveau Château de Herrenchiemsee
Linderhof	Le Château de Linderhof
München	Le Trésor de la Résidence de Munich
	Nymphenburg, Le Château, le Parc et les Pavillons

Neuschwanstein/	Le Château de Neuschwanstein
Hohenschwangau	
Nürnberg	Le Château Impérial de Nuremberg
Würzburg	Wurtzbourg, Le Palais des Princes Évêques et les Jardins

Editions avec résumé français:

| Bayreuth/Wonsees | Felsengarten Sanspareil – Burg Zwernitz |
| München | Englischer Garten München |

Edizioni Italiane:

Herrenchiemsee	Castello di Herrenchiemsee
Linderhof	Castello di Linderhof
München	Nymphenburg, Il Castello, il Parco e i Castelli del Giardino
	Tesoro della Residenz München
Neuschwanstein/	Castello di Neuschwanstein
Hohenschwangau	
Würzburg	La Residenza di Würzburg e il Giardino di Corte

Japanische Ausgaben:

Herrenchiemseee	Schloß Herrenchiemsee
Linderhof	Schloß Linderhof
München	Nymphenburg
Neuschwanstein/	Schloß Neuschwanstein
Hohenschwangau	

Prospekte

Nymphenburger Porzellan, Sammlung Bäuml
Das Bayreuth der Markgräfin Wilhelmine (dt., engl., frz., ital.)
Residenz Kempten (dt., engl.)
Königshaus am Schachen
Schleißheim – eine barocke Residenz
Schloß Rosenau

Museumspädagogische Schriften

Schloß Nymphenburg entdecken

Bildhefte

Heym, Sabine: Das Alte Residenztheater/Cuvilliés-Theater in München, München 1995. DM 15,00 (dt., engl., frz., ital.)

Weitere Veröffentlichungen

Bayerische Verwaltung der staatlichen Schlösser, Gärten und Seen (Hrsg.): **Vierte Festschrift zum Wiederaufbau der Residenz München,** München 1959. DM 5.00

Bayerische Verwaltung der staatlichen Schlösser, Gärten und Seen (Hrsg.): **Journal der Bayerischen Verwaltung der staatlichen Schlösser, Gärten und Seen,** München 1995. DM 10.00

200 Jahre Englischer Garten in München 1789-1989, Offizielle Festschrift, München 1988. DM 4.00

Ermischer, Gerhard: **Schloßarchäologie – Funde zu Schloß Johannisburg in Aschaffenburg,** Aschaffenburg 1996. DM 48.00

Frosien-Leinz, Heike und Ellen Weski (Bearb.): **Das Antiquarium der Münchner Residenz,** Katalog der Skulpturen. 2 Bde., München 1987. (nur im Buchhandel erhältlich)

Helmberger, Werner und Valentin Kockel (Bearb.): **Rom über die Alpen tragen.** Fürsten sammeln antike Architektur. Die Aschaffenburger Korkmodelle (Bestandskatalog), Landshut 1993. DM 35.00, im Buchhandel DM 59.50

Heym, Sabine: **Feenreich und Ritterwelt - die Rosenau als Ort romantisch-literarischen Welterlebens.** Sonderdruck aus „Bayerische Schlösser – Bewahren und Erforschen" (Bayerische Verwaltung der staatlichen Schlösser, Gärten und Seen. Forschungen zur Kunst- und Kulturgeschichte, hrsg. von Gerhard Hojer, Bd. V), München 1996. DM 4.00

Hojer, Gerhard (Hrsg.): **König Ludwig II.-Museum Herrenchiemsee** (Katalog), München 1986. DM 35.00, im Buchhandel DM 48.00

Hojer, Gerhard: **Die Prunkappartements Ludwigs I. im Königsbau der Münchner Residenz,** München 1992. DM 35.00

Hojer, Gerhard (Hrsg.): **Der Italienische Bau.** Materialien und Untersuchungen zur Stadtresidenz Landshut, Landshut 1994. DM 38.00, im Buchhandel DM 74.80

Hojer, Gerhard (Hrsg.): **Bayerische Schlösser - Bewahren und Erforschen,** München 1996. DM 85.00

Krückmann, Peter O. (Bearb.): **Carlo Carlone 1686-1775.** Der Ansbacher Auftrag (Ausstellungskatalog), Landshut 1990. DM 37.00, im Buchhandel DM 79.00

Krückmann, Peter O. (Hrsg.): **Der Himmel auf Erden - Tiepolo in Würzburg,** Bd. I (Ausstellungskatalog), Bd. II (Aufsätze), München, New York 1996. Bd. I DM 39.00, Bd. II DM 49.00, beide Bände DM 79.00

Krückmann, Peter O.: **Heaven on Earth – TIEPOLO – Masterpieces of the Würzburg Years,** München, New York 1996. DM 68.00

Kulturstiftung der Länder in Verbindung mit der Bayerischen Verwaltung der staatlichen Schlösser, Gärten und Seen (Hrsg.): Neues Schloß Bayreuth, Anton Raphael Mengs **»Königin Semiramis erhält die Nachricht vom Aufstand in Babylon«,** München 1995. DM 20.00

Kunz-Ott, Hannelore und Andrea Kluge (Hrsg.): **150 Jahre Feldherrnhalle.** Lebensraum einer Großstadt, München 1994. DM 25.00

Land- und Universitätsbauamt Augsburg im Auftrag der Bayerischen Verwaltung der staatlichen Schlösser, Gärten und Seen (Hrsg.): **Restaurierung Schloß Höchstädt,** Festschrift zur Fertigstellung des 1. Bauabschnitts und zur Eröffnung der Fayencenausstellung am 19. Oktober 1995. DM 6.00

Landbauamt Rosenheim im Auftrag der Bayerischen Verwaltung der staatlichen Schlösser, Gärten und Seen (Hrsg.): **Wasserspiele Herrenchiemsee,** Festschrift 1994 Schloß Herrenchiemsee, München 1994. DM 15.00

Langer, Brigitte: **Die Möbel der Residenz München. Bd. 1.** Die französischen Möbel des 18. Jahrhunderts, hrsg. von Gerhard Hojer und Hans Ottomeyer, München, New York, 1995. DM 98.00, im Buchhandel DM 168.00

Langer, Brigitte und Alexander Herzog von Württemberg: **Die Möbel der Residenz München. Bd. 2.** Die deutschen Möbel des 16. bis 18. Jahrhunderts, hrsg. von Gerhard Hojer und Hans Ottomeyer, München, New York, 1996. DM 98.00, im Buchhandel DM 168.00

Miller, Albrecht (Bearb.): **Bayreuther Fayencen** (Bestandskatalog), Landshut 1994. DM 28.00, im Buchhandel DM 49.80

Mißlbeck-Woesler, Maria: **Die Flora des Englischen Gartens,** München 1986. DM 15.00

Nadler, Stefan (Bearb.): **Julius Exter.** Ein Chiemseemaler in Feldwies, München 1990. DM 7.00

Sangl, Sigrid: **Das Bamberger Hofschreinerhandwerk im 18. Jahrhundert,** München 1990. DM 30.00

Schmid, Elmar D. und Sabine Heym (Bearb.): **Josef Effner 1687-1745.** Bauten für Kurfürst Max Emanuel (Ausstellungskatalog), München 1987. DM 2.00

Schmid, Elmar D. (Bearb.): **Friedrich Wilhelm Pfeiffer 1822-1891.** Maler der Reitpferde König Ludwigs II. (Ausstellungskatalog), Dachau 1988. DM 48.00

Schmid, Elmar D. und Sabine Heym (Bearb.): **Mathias und Anna Gasteiger.** Aus einem Münchner Künstlerleben um 1900 (Ausstellungsbroschüre), Dachau 1985. DM 15.00

Schmid, Elmar D.: **Der Krönungswagen Kaiser Karls VII.** Wahl und Krönung in Frankfurt am Main 1742 (Ausstellungskatalog), Dachau 1992. DM 25.00

Schmid, Elmar D.: **König Ludwig II. im Portrait** (Ausstellungskatalog), Dachau, München 1996. DM 68.00

Schmid, Elmar D.: **Julius Exter** - Unbekannte Werke aus dem Nachlaß seiner Schülerin Olga Fritz-Zetter (Ausstellungskatalog), München 1996. DM 10.00

Schmid, Elmar D.: **Das Exter-Haus**. Ein Künstlersitz am Chiemsee in Übersee-Feldwies, München 1997. DM 10.00

Seelig, Lorenz: **Kirchliche Schätze aus bayerischen Schlössern.** Liturgische Gewänder und Geräte des 16. bis 19. Jahrhunderts (Bestandskatalog), Berlin 1984. DM 25.00

Stierhof, Horst H. (Bearb.): **Das Walhnhaus.** Der italienische Bau der Stadtresidenz Landshut, Landshut 1994. DM 12.00, im Buchhandel DM 16.00

Stierhof, Horst H.: **»das biblisch gemäl«.** 450 Jahre Schloßkapelle Neuburg an der Donau (Ausstellungskatalog), München 1993. DM 5.00

Stierhof, Horst H.: **»das biblisch gemäl«.** Die Kapelle im Ottheinrichsbau des Schlosses Neuburg an der Donau, München 1993. DM 12.00

Störkel, Arno: **Christian Friedrich Carl Alexander.** Der letzte Markgraf von Ansbach-Bayreuth, Ansbach 1995. DM 34.00

Ziffer, Alfred: **Nymphenburger Porzellan.** Die Sammlung Bäuml/Bäuml Collection (Bestandskatalog), Stuttgart 1996. DM 98.00

Preise zzgl. Porto und Verpackung, Bestellungen bitte an:

**Bayerische Verwaltung der staatlichen Schlösser, Gärten und Seen,
Postfach 38 01 20, 80614 München**

Carl von Effner; Plan of the Linderhof Gardens, around 1900